HISTORIC PARIS

Paul Blanchard

Letts **Guides**
Charles Letts and Company Ltd
London, Edinburgh, München and New York

First published 1979
by Charles Letts and Company Limited
Diary House, Borough Road, London
SE1 1DW

ISBN 0 85097 246 9
Printed in Italy by
Coop. Officine Grafiche Firenze
Design and cover by Paul Sharp
Photographs by Raffaello Bencini and
Angelo Hornak
Research by Paolo Zucconi

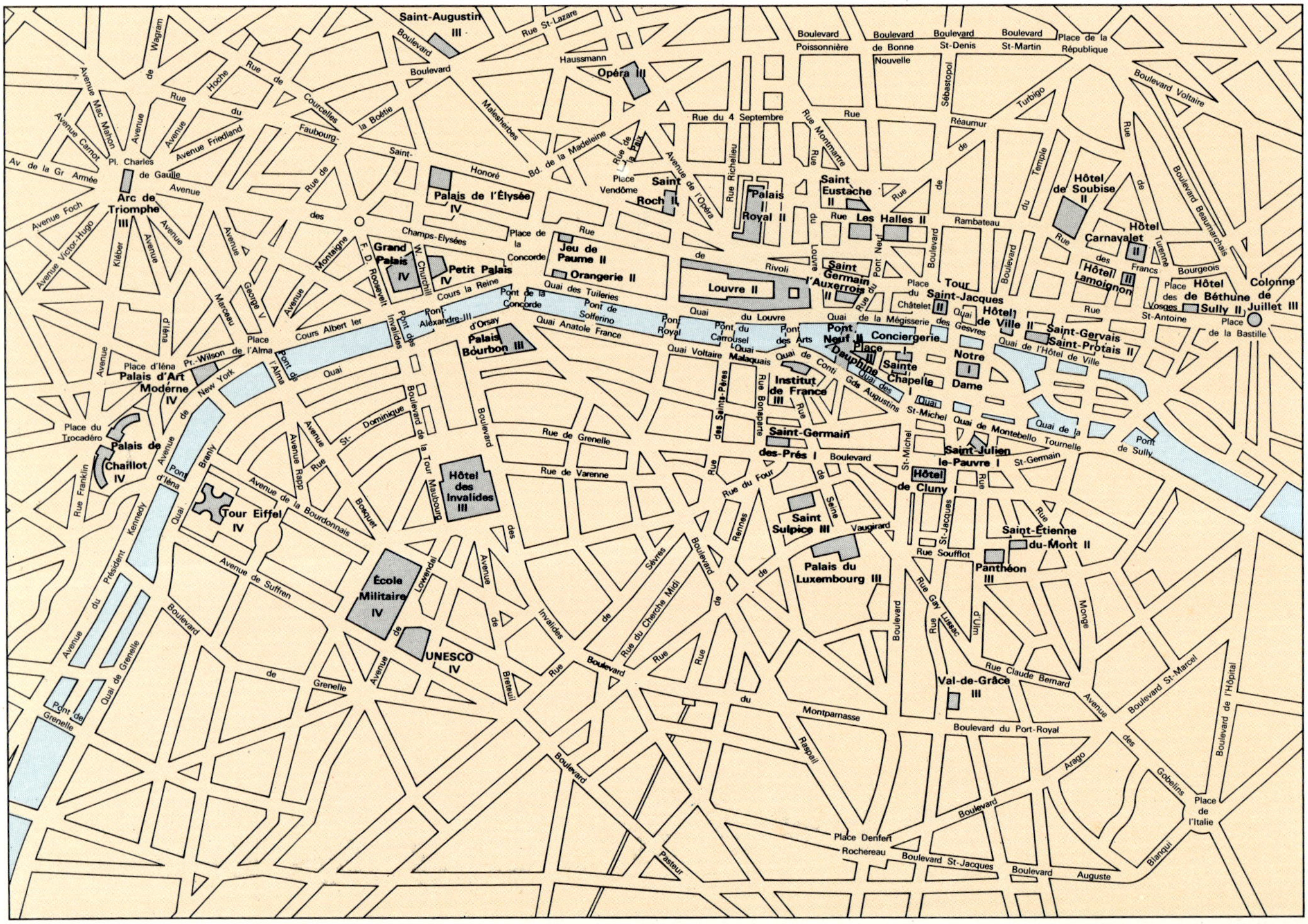

Contents

The apse of the Sainte-Chapelle

General view of Paris looking towards the left bank

Paris before the 16th Century

Paris grew up at the point where the ancient land route from the Rhine district crossed the Seine, which was most easily forded at the Île de la Cité. Lutetia, the fortified Gallic town which later became Paris, was established on this island.

The Romans conquered Lutetia in the 1st century BC (Julius Caesar describes the burning of the city in 52 BC in his *Commentaries*). Under the Pax Romana the city expanded beyond the island (which was much smaller than the present Île de la Cité and was repeatedly flooded by the river) to the Mont Sainte-Geneviève on the left bank. Here a new unfortified Roman town was built according to the rectilinear plan that characterizes most Roman towns. Later a small settlement was begun on the right bank as well.

The Barbarian invasions forced the settlements on the left and right banks to be abandoned in the 3rd century AD. The inhabitants retreated to the original island, which they enclosed in a towerless wall 2.5m thick, built with stones from the Roman monuments. At about the same time (AD 300), the town's name was changed to Paris, derived from the Roman name for the inhabitants of the entire region: the Parisii.

Christianity reached Paris in the 3rd century (a 10th century manuscript refers to St. Denis as the first bishop of Paris, *c* 250). But it was not until Clovis, the leader of the Franks, made the city his capital in 507 that the new religion was officially accepted. In the years that followed, Paris became an important religious centre. Churches and monasteries sprang up on both sides of the Seine. The most important of these included the basilica of Saint-Vincent, in which St Germain, bishop of Paris, was buried in 576, and which later became the abbey of Saint-Germain-des-Prés; and the basilica of Saint-Martin, which later became the priory of Saint-Martin-des-Champs.

In the peaceful years that preceded the Norman invasions, new settlements sprang up outside the walled city. But the Norman siege of 885 and 886 again caused the inhabitants of the river banks to take shelter on the island. Finally, in 911, peace was restored and the woods and swamps around the city were taken into cultivation as farmland. The accession of the Capetian dynasty in 987 united the feudal and ecclesiastical domains which made up Paris. The town grew in importance as the power of the monarchy increased.

In the 11th century, Paris expanded rapidly along both banks of the Seine. As it grew, the city naturally formed into three large 'quarters': the Île de la Cité; the Outre-Petit-Pont or left bank; and the Outre-Grand-Pont or right bank, also called the 'Ville'. The left bank became the centre of intellectual activity. Here the university was formed by a group of masters and students whose association was recognized by Philip Augustus in 1200. The right bank became the centre of commercial activity (mainly trade and transportation). It contained the market and in the 12th century it was surrounded by a separate wall.

The 13th century was called the century of Saint-Louis, for it was dominated by the long reign of Louis IX (1223-1270). During this period the gothic style developed splendidly in France and spread throughout Europe, to the coasts of the Mediterranean and the threshold of Asia. At the same time, Paris became one of the leading intellectual centres in Europe. In the second half of the 13th century and throughout the 14th century, numerous colleges including the one established by Robert Sorbon, called the Sorbonne after his death, were founded on the left bank of the Seine.

The 14th century witnessed the climax of expansion and power in medieval Paris. The population increased rapidly, making Paris the largest city in Europe. A wealthy middle class, led by the *marchands de l'eau*, the river traders' guild, acquired new power as a consequence of the importance of commercial traffic on the Seine but, though the middle class won privileges, government of the city was reserved to the king and administered by his representative, the provost of Paris.

Today almost nothing remains of the medieval city. A long series of modifications, beginning during the reign of Francis I and continuing into the 20th century greatly changed Paris. The Louvre, originally part of Philip Augustus' fortifications, was reconstructed in 1528; a new city wall was planned, but it was not built until the following century, during the reign of Louis XIII, and then only on the right bank. The first examples of renaissance art and architecture appeared.

When Henry II became King in 1547 the Renaissance was in full flower. The aristocracy continued to build monumental houses on the right bank, a process which had begun during the 12th century, but the king urged that the façades of the new houses be made of stone, like the renaissance palaces of Italy, and not of wood and plaster. The remodelling of the Louvre continued and Catherine de Médicis began the construction of the Jardin des Tuileries in 1564. The renaissance spirit of Henry's court spread throughout the city, and manners and tastes in Paris became more refined. Quays were constructed along the Seine and an effort was made to bring the streets into orderly alignment. The Pont Neuf, the first classical bridge to be built on the Seine, was begun in 1577 and completed under Henry IV. Paris began to reflect the character of the absolute monarchy.

The tourist who is interested in the ancient past of Paris usually turns to the **Île de la Cité.** Guidebooks may

The Conciergerie along the Seine

lead him to believe that he will find Gallic or Roman monuments on the island. But the remnants of ancient Paris which existed on the Île de la Cité were destroyed in the 19th century to make way for new buildings erected under Louis Philippe and Napoleon III.

The palace of the Roman governors, which later became the residence of the Merovingian kings, was constructed on the site of what is now the Palais de Justice. In the 13th century Louis IX constructed a new royal palace and the Sainte-Chapelle which, together with the Conciergerie and the cathedral of Notre-Dame, has survived.

From the centre of the Pont au Change, which was originally lined with goldsmiths' shops and exchange banks, the Île de la Cité appears to be divided in two by the Boulevard du Palais. The Palais de Justice stands on the right side of the Boulevard; the Tribunal de Commerce and the Préfecture de Police on the left.

The Sainte-Chapelle and the **Conciergerie** have both been absorbed by the massive Palais de Justice, which was built in the 19th century. The original Conciergerie, erected by Philip the Fair in the 14th century and restored in the 19th by Viollet-le-Duc, occupies the north-east corner of the present building, between the Boulevard du Palais and the Quai de l'Horloge. When Charles V moved the royal residence to the Louvre in 1358, the Conciergerie became the seat of parliament, then the supreme court of the kingdom. From the 16th century onward it was used as a prison: during the Revolution of 1789 it held the 2600 prisoners who were tried by the revolutionary court and beheaded. The most famous of Conciergerie prisoners was Marie Antoinette who was placed here under the closest surveillance on 1 August 1793. It was from here that she was led out to her trial on 14 October and her execution on 16 October of the same year.

The façade of the Palais de Justice with the Sainte-Chapelle on the left

The Salle des Gens d'Armes in the Conciergerie

The adjacent buildings, which include the Tribunal Civil and the Cour du Mai, were constructed between 1786 and 1853. The first room we enter after crossing the outer courtyard is the **Salle des Gardes,** a large 14th-century hall divided into two broad aisles with gothic cross vaults 6.9 m high. The room was extensively restored in the 19th century: the decorative capitals of the massive piers are not original.

The adjacent **Salle des Gens d'Armes,** or great lower hall, is a splendid example of the gothic conception of interior space. It is rivalled only by Mont Saint-Michel and the papal palace in Avignon. The hall, whose end bay (the Rue de Paris where poor prisoners were held) is separated from the rest by a large gate, is 63m long and 27m wide. Columns and piers divide the room into four aisles with gothic cross vaults. Originally designed as the meal hall for the soldiers, servants and guards who populated the palace, the room now houses a small collection of decorative sculpture.

A passageway leads from the Salle des Gens d'Armes to the **Cuisines de Saint-Louis,** at the base of the spiral staircase which once led to the great upper hall (destroyed by fire in 1618). Four large fireplaces occupied the corners of this 14th-century kitchen, in which meals were prepared for the entire palace staff.

From the Boulevard du Palais one enters the monumental **Cour du Mai,** built between 1783 and 1786 by the architects Desmaisons and Antoine. On the right side of this courtyard is the square **Tour de l'Horloge,** which dates from the time of John the Good who had the clock placed on it in 1334. A three-bayed passageway beneath the arcade that defines the left side of the courtyard leads to the cloister of the **Sainte-Chapelle.** The original cloister was larger, with the chapel as its centre. The present plan is a 19th-century reconstruction.

The chapel was constructed be-

A detail of Christ and two angels from the decoration of the Sainte-Chapelle

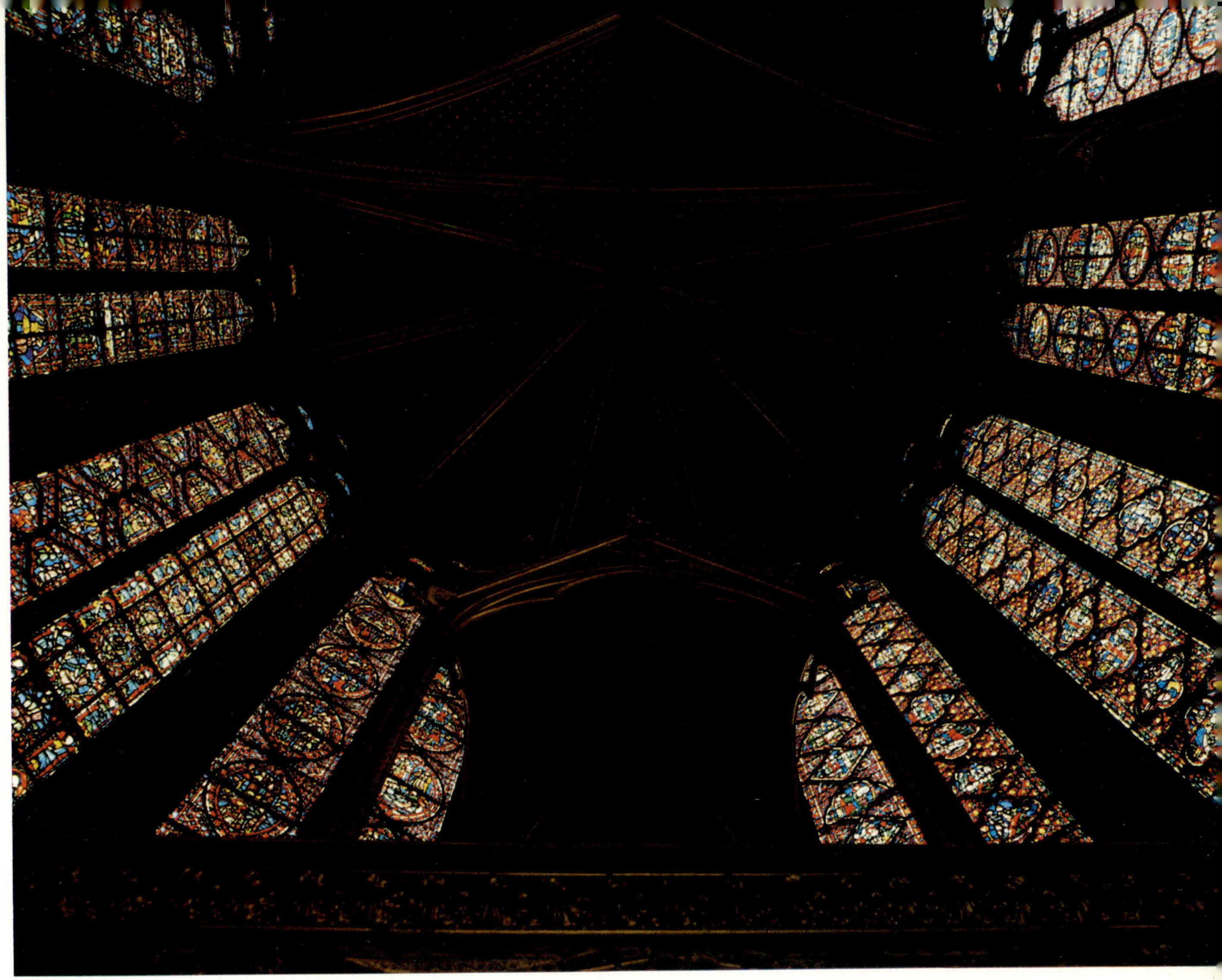

Interior of the apse of the Sainte-Chapelle

tween 1241 and 1248 by Louis IX. It was built to accommodate the reliquary containing the Crown of Thorns and the fragment of the True Cross which had been brought to Paris from the Holy Land. A synthesis of the highest achievement of 13th-century builders and craftsmen, the chapel is one of the most significant works of gothic art.

The building consists of an upper chapel (for use by the king and his court) and a lower one (to be used by the servants). This design gives it an unexpected vertical thrust despite its modest size. Superimposed arcades on the façade correspond to the two chapels.

The upper chapel is 20m high. It is supported from the outside by a system of simple buttresses. Inside, a continuous arcaded baseboard runs around the lower portion of the walls. Two deep niches below the windows of the fourth bay interrupt the baseboard: here, on either side of the chapel, the royal family stood during the celebration of mass.

The slender columns which hold up the vaulted ceiling bear 14th-century statues of the Apostles (many of which have been replaced by copies). Between them, fifteen large stained-glass windows rise from the arcaded baseboard to the arches of the vaults. These windows, each over 15m high and 4m wide, are decorated with illustrations of bible stories. Together they constitute a continuous glass wall, a courageous feat of gothic engineering. The enormous amount of light the windows admit tends to unify the interior of the chapel, dissolving the disparity between glass and stone: the two materials blend together to create the effect of luminous, aerial space for which the Sainte-Chapelle is famous.

Detail of the exterior of the Sainte-Chapelle

Façade of Notre-Dame

Notre-Dame, the portal of St Anne

The cathedral of **Notre-Dame** is one of the masterpieces of medieval French architecture. Seen from below, the upward thrust and rhythmic harmony of its walls create a dramatic effect which invariably impresses the visitor. Nevertheless, Notre-Dame as it appears today is largely the product of the consolidation, restoration, additions and modifications of the 19th-century architect, Viollet-Le-Duc.

Notre-Dame occupies a crucial point in the evolution of the gothic system. One might say that it is a prototype of all the innovations which follow it. Its plan, conceived by Bishop Maurice de Sully in 1160, offered its architects (the earliest of whom are unknown) a wide range of possibilities for developing the system of static forces that typify gothic architecture. The construction of the cathedral began in 1163 and work continued until 1345. Its builders translated the technical knowledge they acquired during the

Notre-Dame, external gallery and gargoyles

course of construction into new and increasingly complex structural achievements. For instance, they directed the weight of the large vaults of the ceiling onto the buttresses of the side-aisles, using arches which span the aisle roof and abut the upper nave wall (flying buttresses). This enabled them to eliminate the massive walls which would have been necessary to bear the weight of the stone ceiling. The thrust imposed by the vaults on these load-bearing elements (which are visible from outside the cathedral) is overwhelmingly downward. But the eye reads this movement in reverse, giving the whole structure a strong sense of upward motion.

The same feeling of upward thrust pervades the interior of the cathedral, which is 130m long, 48m wide at the transept and 35m high. Heavy columns divide the interior into a central nave and four aisles. The light enters through the large stained glass windows of the apse and through the large rose windows at the ends of the nave and transept. The rose window of the nave (1220-1225) includes a representation of the Virgin Mary surrounded by the Months and the Signs of the Zodiac. It still contains parts of the original 13th-century stained glass. The best preserved stained glass is that of the rose window in the south transept (1255).

opposite page Notre-Dame, the right aisle

Notre-Dame, detail of the flying buttresses

Notre-Dame, the vaulted ceiling in the ambulatory

The window is 12m in diameter. It depicts the Virgin and Child surrounded by Old Testament prophets, judges, patriarchs and kings. The rose window in the north transept shows Christ surrounded by martyrs, saints, the Apostles and the Wise and Foolish Virgins. Two oculi (circular openings in the wall) with smaller windows, brought to light by Viollet-le-Duc, are visible from the sanctuary. A 14th-century statue of Our Lady of Paris (Notre-Dame de Paris) stands on the column at the south side of the entrance to the sanctuary.

A Roman temple stood on the site of Notre-Dame in pre-Christian times. It was replaced by an early Christian basilica, which was in turn demolished to make way for the medieval cathedral. The sanctuary, ambulatory, nave and transept of the present structure were constructed between 1163 and 1200. The nave façade and its two rectangular towers were begun in the 12th century and were completed in 1245. The nave chapels were built between 1230 and 1240; the sanctuary chapels, between 1296 and 1320. Jean de Chelles began the façade of the north transept in 1250. Pierre de Montreuil began that of the south transept in 1258. The apse, with its magnificent system of flying buttresses, was completed in 1344, under the direction of Jean de Ravy.

The exterior of the cathedral bears a rich adornment of sculptural decoration, though many of the original 13th-century pieces have been lost or destroyed and some have been replaced by modern copies. An arcade containing statues of the kings of Israel runs across the façade, above the three monumental portals. The original statues, thought to represent the kings of France, were destroyed in 1793 and replaced by copies in the 19th century.

The central zone of the principal façade contains the large rose

Notre-Dame, detail of the portal of the Last Judgment

Notre-Dame, detail from the portal of the Virgin

window flanked by two mullioned windows. A second arcade, decorated with a delicate network of blind tracery, runs across the top of the façade between the two rectangular towers. A trumeau at the central portal bears a statue of Christ, and statues of the Wise and Foolish Virgins and of the Apostles. Relief panels depicting the Virtues and Vices flank the double doors. Above, the tympanum contains a representation of the Last Judgment. Heaven and Hell are depicted on the surface of the arch.

The trumeau of the south portal bears a statue of the Virgin and Child. The months are represented on the door posts and saints, prophets, patriarchs and angels on the chamfers and arch. A relief depicting the Death and Coronation of the Virgin occupies the tympanum.

Kings, queens, patriarchs and angels flank the north portal. Scenes from the lives of the Virgin and St Anne occupy the tympanum.

The Virgin and Child appear too on the trumeau of the north transept portal (the Porte du Cloître). The tympanum contains scenes from the lives of the Virgin and the deacon Theophilus, the precursor of all those who sell their souls to the devil. The small garden or Porte Rouge (1270) bears another relief of the Coronation of the Virgin and kneeling figures thought to represent Louis IX and Margaret of Provence.

Scenes from the life of St Stephen decorate the tympanum of the south transept portal (Porte de Saint-Étienne). Relief medallions depicting student life flank the doors.

The **Latin Quarter** is the traditional home of the University of Paris. Its boundaries are rather vague; it can be taken to extend roughly in a rectangle from the south bank of the Seine at the Île de la Cité to the summit of Mont Sainte-Geneviève. It became a major centre of learning in the 12th century, when teachers and students from the

ARMANDVS·IOANNES·CARD·DVX·RICHELIVS·SORBONAE·PROVIS·R
AEDIFICAVIT·DOMVM·ET·EXALTAVIT·TEMPLVM·S·DOMINO·MDCXLI

The tomb of Cardinal Richelieu in the church of the Sorbonne

cathedral school of Notre-Dame moved away from the Île de la Cité to live in the country on the left bank. Philip Augustus united the numerous colleges he founded to form the university at the beginning of the 13th century. The university developed rapidly as a famous intellectual centre, attracting students from all parts of Europe and from Asia Minor and Africa as well. Many leading philosophers and theologians, including St Thomas Aquinas and St Bonaventure, taught there.

The University was founded in 1253 by Robert de Sorbon, confessor to Louis IX (St Louis). Until the revolution it was the centre of theological studies as well as the University of Paris. During the Hundred Years' War the Sorbonne recognized Henry V of England as king of France. The bishop of the Sorbonne, Peter Cauchon, played an important part in the trial of Joan of Arc at Rouen as he once again sided with the English and helped secure Joan's condemnation.

Cardinal Richelieu had the entire complex rebuilt during the 17th century under the direction of the architect Lemercier. The only building today of this reconstruction is the church where the great cardinal is buried. His tomb, a magnificent creation in white marble, was built by Girardon in 1694.

Today the Quarter is still a centre of student life, although the university itself is housed in buildings in all parts of Paris.

The church of **Saint-Julien-le-Pauvre** occupies a small garden directly south of the Seine from Notre-Dame. Although it was built at about the same time as Notre-Dame, very little remains of the original structure. The romanesque-gothic interior is divided into three aisles on piers with interesting decorated capitals. The central portion of the apse contains notable cross vaults and is lighted by two orders of windows. The church is

The church of the Sorbonne

The church of Saint-Julien-le-Pauvre

occupied by the Malachites, Greek Catholics, and mass is sung there on Sundays and feast days according to Byzantine rites.

The narrow, winding streets of the Latin Quarter are among the oldest in Paris. Rue du Fouarre, originally called Rue du Feurre, derives its name from the straw on which the first students who migrated to the left bank sat while attending lessons. Rue Saint-Jacques, which leads from the Île de la Cité to the slopes of Mont Sainte-Geneviève, stands in clear contrast to the narrow side streets. It was the major highway to the south used by the Gauls and the Romans. In the Middle Ages it was the road followed by pilgrims bound for the religious sanctuaries of Spain: at the beginning of the road is the church of **Saint-Séverin.**

Originally a romanesque structure, the church of Saint-Séverin was

Interior of the church of Saint-Séverin

rebuilt in the gothic style over a 300-year period ranging from the 13th to the 16th century. It has a nave, four side aisles, and a small sanctuary. There is no transept. The original structure was a three-aisled basilica. The aisle on the southern side was begun in 1413; that on the northern side, in 1450. The apse was constructed between 1489 and 1496 and the chapels added between 1498 and 1520.

The 13th-century main portal was transferred to Saint-Séverin from the demolished church of Saint-Pierre-aux-Boeufs in 1837.

The church is 50m long, 34m wide and 17m high; these dimensions emphasise the unusual breadth of the double ambulatory. The columns and vaults of the ambulatory are particularly interesting: the ribs of the double arches fall back on the columns, creating a tree-like effect.

Entrance to the courtyard of the Hôtel de Cluny

Room IV in the Musée de Cluny

Near the intersection of Rue Saint-Jacques and the Boulevard Saint-Germain is one of the few extant examples of late medieval secular architecture in Paris: the **Hôtel de Cluny.**

The site of the Hôtel was originally occupied by a Roman public bath. It became the property of the kings of France. It was then donated to the powerful Benedictine order of Cluny in the 14th century. The abbot, Jacques d'Amboise, constructed the Hôtel between 1485 and 1500 as a residence for abbots during their visits to Paris.

No one has ever tried to reconstruct the monument's history and to distinguish the original structure from later additions and modifications is difficult, as the changes it has undergone are not fully documented.

A stained-glass window from the Sainte-Chapelle in the Musée de Cluny

The Hôtel de Cluny was opened in 1844 as a museum of art and life in medieval Paris. The collection is distributed throughout the building in twenty rooms. It is divided into parts which correspond to the various guilds active in Paris during the Middle Ages. It is of social, as well as artistic and historic interest for it provides a vivid image of life in the medieval city.

In Room IV, one of the more beautiful rooms, tapestries depicting *La Vie Seigneuriale* create a refined picture of courtly life in the last years of the Middle Ages. Four of the twelve statues of Apostles (1245-1248) from the Sainte-Chapelle are on exhibition in Room IX. The celebrated series of tapestries representing the *Dame à la Licorne* occupies an entire room on the upper floor (Room XI).

A scene from *La Dame à la Licorne* in the Musée de Cluny

Detail of the vault ribbing in the Chapel of the Hôtel de Cluny

In the Chapel, a pure and balanced example of flamboyant gothic architecture, hangs a suite of tapestries 45m long, with scenes from the legend of St Stephen.

The grandiose Roman baths of the 2nd and 3rd century, which adjoin the eastern part of the **Hôtel, house a** collection of Roman objects found in Paris. The vaulted *frigidarium* is 200m long, 14m wide and 14m high. Recent archaeological excavations have revealed the baths in their entirety.

Further up the Boulevard Saint Germain is the church of **Saint-Germain-des-Prés.** St Germain, the founder of the original construction, was bishop of Paris in the 6th century. He was buried in 576 in the basilica whose construction he had helped to bring about.

The Benedictine monastery of Saint-Germain-des-Prés grew up around the church in the 8th century. It soon became a large community on the outskirts of medieval Paris. It remained one of the city's more powerful monasteries throughout and after the Middle Ages. As a result of the Revolution, however, its political power was drastically cut back.

A romanesque church built during the 11th and 12th centuries replaced the early Christian basilica of Saint-Germain. Today the church is the oldest, and consequently the most extensively altered, in Paris. Some elements of the original romanesque structure remain: the tower dates from the first half of the 11th century and the nave from the second half. The gothic sanctuary was completed in the 12th century.

The interior is 65m long, 21m wide and 19m high. It includes a nave, two side aisles, a transept and a deep sanctuary with an ambulatory and radial chapels. The composite effect of the romanesque nave, its wooden roof and the series of piers with attached colomns is barely discernible beneath the 19th-century recon-

The Roman baths in the Hôtel de Cluny

The church of Saint-Germain-des-Prés

struction. The original capitals of the columns are today in the museum of the Hôtel de Cluny.

The remains of the gothic monastery – the refectory (1234-1244) and the Chapel of the Virgin (1248-1255) – attributed to Pierre de Montreuil, are visible in the small garden north of the church. The head of a woman, sculpted by Pablo Picasso in homage to the poet Guillaume Apollinaire, is also to be found in the garden.

Picasso's *Homage to Apollinaire* in the garden of Saint-Germain-des-Prés

The apse of Notre-Dame

Renaissance and the Beginnings of Neoclassicism

From Louis IX to Henry IV, the kings of France had no fixed residence. They lived mainly in the castles of the Loire and they rarely visited the capital.

Violent religious struggles shook the city in their absence. The spread of the Protestant faith caused a bitter reaction amongst Parisian Catholics, which culminated in the famous massacre of St Bartholomew's Day, 24 August 1572.

The conflict grew steadily worse and a series of political errors on the part of Henry III led to the king's expulsion from Paris in 1588. His successor, Henry of Navarre (Henry IV), laid siege to the city. He was finally admitted in 1594, after having abjured the Protestant faith.

16th-century Paris was still a rural agglomerate. Vast agricultural lands surrounded the city and a large community of farmers and agricultural workers grew up within its walls. Henry II forbade the construction of new buildings outside the city walls claiming that they would be difficult to defend, but his intention was in fact to halt the process of extra-urban development which would increase the population exempt from taxation.

Paris continued to expand despite the king's will. The growth of the suburbs of Saint-Germain and Saint-Honoré at the west end of the city led to the erection of a new, more extensive wall and to the construction of a new bridge at the western end of the Île de la Cité. The building of the Pont Neuf was the most important public project of the time. It accompanied the construction of the Cour Carrée, the Tuileries Palace and the Grande Galerie which joined the Tuileries to the Louvre.

The Renaissance reached Paris after the Italian campaigns of Charles VIII, Louis XII and Francis I. Close artistic ties continued to exist between France and Italy throughout the 16th and 17th centuries and elements deriving from the Italian Renaissance gradually penetrated Parisian architecture, largely in the works of the architect Pierre Lescot and the sculptor Jean Goujon.

The urban projects of the great French monarchs of the 17th and 18th centuries drastically changed the appearance of Paris. Much of the medieval city was destroyed to make way for the *places royales*, open spaces in the centre, free from traffic, architecturally controlled and designed to glorify the reign and to confer dignity on the urban environment.

From the reign of Henry IV to the First Empire, a constant population increase in the city, connected with the establishment of the absolute monarchy and the growth of Paris' importance in Europe, caused extensive expansion. This led to the growth of the city beyond the walls and to the re-use of parks and open spaces for building. At the same time several wide boulevards were constructed, both in the old city and in the new zones of expansion. In 1666 work began on the Champs-Elysées, under the direction of Le Nôtre. Louis XIV completed the Cours de Vincennes and the Hôtel des Invalides and ordered the construction of the Palace of Versailles, which caused the city to expand towards the west.

The 17th-century architect Christophe Marie was the first to propose developing a section of Paris solely for profit. His project consisted of joining two small islands to form a new quarter linked by bridges to the banks of the Seine. The new island was named the **Île Saint-Louis** in honour of Louis IX.

The Île Saint-Louis failed to yield the financial rewards its planners had hoped for. Nevertheless, its homogeneous architecture was a success as a feat of urban planning.

The character of life on the island is semi-provincial. The Métro does not touch it. Only one bus (No 67) passes through it. There are no taxis, and it is considered a rather sophisticated place to live.

The quays of the Île Saint-Louis offer several striking views of the city. The apse of Notre-Dame is visible from the Quai de Béthune and the heart of the now-destroyed medieval town, which extended from the Tour Saint-Jacques to the Marais, can be seen from the Quai d'Orléans and the Quai de Bourbon.

There are many 17th-century mansions on the Île Saint-Louis, untouched and unsurrounded by modern progress, such as the **Hôtel Lambert** where, at one time or another, Voltaire, George Sand and Prince Czartoryski lived (it now houses many works of art).

The term *marais* indicates marshland which can be reclaimed and cultivated. The stagnant pool which the Seine's flood waters left on the right bank opposite the Île Saint-Louis caused this area to be called the Marais.

The area was first used for agricultural purposes by the Knights of the Temple in the Middle Ages, but at the end of the 17th century became a residential quarter, inhabited by the aristocracy, notably by the Valois. The Marais today is an opulent extension of the Île Saint-Louis. It contains numerous outstanding examples of mannerist architecture, rare in Paris, where the transition from gothic to neoclassical was rapid and complete.

The church of **Saint-Étienne-du-Mont,** near the Panthéon, forms a bridge in style between Parisian gothic monuments and the renaissance buildings encountered on the right bank between the Marais and the Louvre.

The 13th-century church was completely rebuilt between the 15th and 17th centuries. The work of reconstruction began in 1492 and was completed in 1622 with the erection of the façade, a mixture of gothic and renaissance motifs. Restorations and reconstructions have continued until the present day.

Interior of the church of Saint-Étienne-du-Mont

The interior includes a nave, two aisles and a transept and chancel, both with ambulatory. The elegant pulpit (1521-1545) is attributed to Philibert de l'Orme but is more probably the work of Antoine Beaucorps. It is the only one of its kind to have survived the destruction of the pulpits in Parisian churches during the 17th and 18th centuries.

In the Marais, on the Rue Saint Antoine is the **Hôtel de Béthune-Sully.** The role of the architect-statesman Jean Androuet du Cerceau in the construction of this Hôtel is uncertain; that he bought the building in 1634, ten years after it was begun, is, however, widely known.

Large bas-reliefs representing the Seasons and the Elements decorate

Detail of the façade of the church of Saint-Étienne

Allegorical figures on the courtyard walls of the Hôtel de Béthune-Sully

the walls of the main courtyard. Autumn and Winter are depicted on the main façade; Air and Fire on the facade of the left wing and Earth and Water on that of the right wing. Spring and Summer appear on the asymmetrical façade of the rear wall.

The small garden contains the interesting **Petit-Sully,** which was originally designed as a hothouse for lemon trees.

The large square called **Place des Vosges,** off the Rue des Francs Bourgeois, is the prototype of the *places royales* conceived by Henry IV as centres of urban activity.

The Place des Vosges was completed in 1612, two years after Henry's death. Its regular plan – a rectangle 140 by 127m in size, divided into four equal parts by a major (north-south) and a minor (east-west) axis – and the uniform and symmetrical buildings that surround it typify the pure, rational forms of the Parisian Renaissance. The combined use of red brick and white stone, which appears here for the first time, becomes characteristic of architecture from the period of Louis XIII.

From the time of its completion Place des Vosges became the centre of the elegant life of Paris. It remained so for more than a century. At No 6 is the **House of Victor Hugo,** which houses a complete collection of all editions of his works, an extensive library of works written about Hugo as well as some 350 drawings by Hugo himself.

The Hôtel de Béthune-Sully

Place des Vosges

Hôtel Carnavalet

The Apotheosis of Napoleon in the Musée Carnavalet

Also on the Rue des Francs Bourgeois, although the entrance is on Rue de Sévigny, is the **Hôtel Carnavalet,** which one enters through a monumental door designed by Pierre Lescot in 1544 for Jacques de Ligneris, then president of Parliament. The keystone bears a carved figure of Plentitude which was later changed into a carnival mask, an allusion to the name, Carnavalet. (Carnavalet is in turn a corruption of Kernevenay. The name derives from the Breton king of Kernevenay, whose widow lived in the palace at the end of the 16th century). The keystone and the other doorway reliefs were carved by Jean Gujon. Gujon and Lescot worked together on several other monuments of the Parisian Renaissance, notably the Louvre and the Fontaine des Innocents.

The original Hôtel Carnavalet was composed of a central structure and two wings, but it has been altered by various attempts at restoration. The façade of the central structure bears large bas-reliefs of the Seasons and Signs of the Zodiac executed in 1550 by Goujon's workshop. Goujon himself carved the genii on the door at the end of the left wing and the figures of Authority and Fame on the keystone of the door near the courtyard.

The Hôtel houses a museum dedicated to history and the decorative arts. There are rooms which illustrate Parisian iconography from the 16th to the 19th centuries, the reign of Louis XIV, the Napoleonic period, the Restoration and the July monarchy, etc.

Further along the Rue des Francs Bourgeois is the **Hôtel de Soubise,** which now houses the Archives Nationales and the Musée de l'Histoire de France. The richly decorated 17th-century rooms contain documents relating to the history of the country from the Merovingians to the Congress of Vienna.

Coysevox's statue of Louis XIV in the Hôtel Carnavalet

The Hôtel Lamoignon

The **Hôtel Lamoignon,** on Rue de Montmorency, is one of the largest houses of the old Marais. It was built in 1584 and Henry II's daughter, the Duchess of Angoulême, enlarged the original structure at the end of the 16th century. It was further altered during later restorations.

The courtyard façade, with corinthian columns which rise to the cornice, is the earliest well-preserved example of the so-called colossal style.

The church of Saint-Gervais-Saint-Protais

Detail of the interior of Saint-Gervais-Saint-Protais

The buttressed apse of the church of **Saint-Gervais-Saint-Protais,** in the Place Saint Gervais near the Hôtel de Ville, is visible from the Rue des Barres. A 6th-century basilica originally occupied the site, but the present structure was built between 1494 and 1657, a classic example of flamboyant gothic architecture.

The church is entered at the left of the apse. The interior retains the three-aisled plan of the early Christian basilica. It is 73.6m deep and 34.6m wide. The nave vaults are nearly 26m high. The Jacquet brothers carved the sculptural decoration of the large, protruding keystone in the Chapel of the Virgin at the end of the apse. The stone is 2m wide and projects 1.15m from the wall.

The tripartite doric façade (1616-1621), surmounted by a triangular ionic and corinthian pediment, was designed by Clément Métezeau.

The **Hôtel de Ville** is the seat of the municipal administration of the city of Paris. As early as 1357 there was on this site the Maison des Piliers, which housed the municipality. When this building became too small, Francis I ordered a new, larger construction to be built in the same place; work was begun in 1533 and was not completed until the reign of Henry IV. During the Revolution the Hôtel de Ville housed a revolutionary committee; in 1794 Robespierre was arrested in this building and executed the following day. In 1800 Napoleon reorganised the administration of the city and enlarged the Hôtel de Ville, and, still later, Haussmann quadrupled the area of the square around the building, demolishing all the old houses around it. In 1870 the Third Republic was proclaimed here, but the following year, during the Commune, the Hôtel de Ville was burnt down. The building we see today was built between 1874 and 1882 by the architects Ballu and Deperthes.

On the exterior of the Hôtel are 136 statues of famous Parisians; the equestrian statue in front of the south façade is of Étienne Marcel (1310-1358), the first mayor of the city.

The **Tour Saint-Jacques,** on the Rue de Rivoli between the Hôtel de Ville and the Louvre, is 52m high and originally stood beside the south portal of the demolished church of Saint-Jacques-la-Boucherie. It was built during the reign of Francis I, between 1508 and 1522. It is now used as a meteorological observatory.

On the cornice of the tower are

The Tour Saint-Jacques and the monument to the Republic

The Pont Neuf

statues of St James and the symbols of the Evangelists. At the entrance to the tower there is a statue of the philosopher and mathematician Blaise Pascal (1623-1662), who carried out some important research on the density of air here in 1648.

Continuing along the Rue de Rivoli, the area to the right is the area of **Les Halles,** where the open-air food market was held until 1968. Although the markets have now been moved out of the centre of the city, the area still has its charm.

The church of **Saint-Eustache,** immediately to the north of Les Halles, was built between 1532 and 1637, and is an interesting example of how a prevalently gothic structure can absorb many renaissance elements. The plan and the basic architectural principles of this church are gothic, but the decoration belongs to the Renaissance.

Many famous people are buried in this church, such as Molière, Madame de Pompadour and the composer Rameau. In 1855, the composer Hector Berlioz gave the first performance of his *Te Deum* on the organ of Saint-Eustache, and, in 1866, Franz Liszt performed his *Messe de Gran* here.

On the way back to the Rue de Rivoli, it is worthwhile to stop off in the Place des Innocents, off the Rue Pierre Lescot, to have a look at the **Fontaine des Innocents,** built in 1549 by Jean Gujon on a design by Pierre Lescot.

Off the Rue de Rivoli, to the south, is the Rue du Pont Neuf at the end of which is the **Pont Neuf,** the oldest and most famous of the bridges which cross the Seine. Its construction, begun in 1517, was interrupted in 1589 by the death of Henry III and was resumed at Henry IV's wish in 1598. The last stones were laid in 1606.

The formal grace and linear beauty of the Pont Neuf are the chief reasons for its fame. The first paved bridge in Paris, the Pont Neuf afforded an unprecedented view of the city and the river. It was thus a key to a new vision of the city, a vision which the urban planners who changed the face of Paris in the 18th and 19th centuries could not ignore.

Jacques Callot and Stefano della Bella were the first of a long line of artists to paint the Pont Neuf.

The Pont Neuf crosses the Île de la Cité at the apex of the triangular **Place Dauphine,** the first of Henry IV's *places royales* to be completed.

The president of parliament transformed the king's garden in 1607 into a symmetrically ordered triangle closed on three sides by stone and brick buildings with identical façades

The church of Saint-Germain-l'Auxerrois

on all fronts. Only a few buildings today retain their original appearance. A large underground parking lot has been built beneath the square and the building which formed the third side of the triangle has been destroyed, revealing the Palais the Justice.

Returning towards the Louvre, in the Place du Louvre, is the church of **Saint-Germain-l'Auxerrois,** the church of the Louvre and the parochial church of the kings of France. The bells of this church rang out the alarm on the night of 24 August 1572 (St Bartholomew's Day), signalling the massacre in Paris of scores of Protestants.

The romanesque bell tower is the oldest element of the church, which was completed in the 16th century. Although it was extensively altered in the 18th and 19th centuries, the church remains an important example of extravagant gothic architecture.

The lower part of the façade ends in a three-bayed late gothic porch, built by Jean Gaussel between 1435 and 1439. The main portal dates from the 13th century. The nave, four side aisles, the transept and transept portals are part of the 15th-century building. The choir and apse, whose original appearance has been completely changed by restorations, date from the 13th century.

The interior is 78m long and 39m wide. The rose window and the two windows of the southern transept still contain the orignal 12th-century stained glass. The windows of the northern transept date from the 16th century.

From the courtyard of the adjacent city school one can admire a profusely decorated renaissance door, which leads to the apse.

Many of the artists who lived in the Louvre in the 18th century are buried in Saint-Germain-l'Auxerrois: the architects Gabriel, Soufflot and Le Vau, the painters Boucher, Nattier and Chardin and the poet Malherbe.

The size and the mass of the **Louvre,** which extends between the Seine and the Rue de Rivoli for about half a mile, its location near the centre of the city and the museum it houses constitute an unequalled attraction for the visitor.

The history of the Louvre extends from the 13th to the 19th century. The building was originally conceived by Philip Augustus as a fortress to defend Paris from the west. Charles V made it his royal residence an the 14th century, and in 1546 Francis I demolished the old fortress and commissioned Pierre Lescot to construct a renaissance

The Colonnade of the Louvre

The Winged Victory of Samothrace

palace in its place. Work continued under Henry II, but was halted by the king's death, leaving the southwestern part of the present Cour Carrée incomplete. In 1563 Catherine de Médicis began construction of a palace in the grounds of the Jardin des Tuileries, which she linked to the Louvre by a long wing along the Seine (this and the Cour Carrée make up the Vieux Louvre). The Cour Carrée was completed and its eastern façade (the celebrated Colonnade) was constructed under Louis XIII and Louis XIV. The work was interrupted in 1674, to be resumed in the 19th century by Charles Percier and Pierre-François-Léonard Fontaine, the architects of Napoleon I. They began the northern wing (the Nouveau Louvre), the mirror image of that constructed by Catherine de Médicis. Ludovico Visconti and Hector Lefuel carried the project to completion under Napoleon III. The Louvre assumed its present form when the Tuileries Palace was destroyed, during the Paris Commune.

The vast edifice of the Vieux Louvre is best seen from a point near the Pont Neuf. The southern façade of the Cour Carrée, designed by Louis Perrault in 1668, is visible at the extreme right and the Petite Galerie, begun in 1566 by order of Catherine de Médicis, completed under Henry IV and reconstructed by Le Vau, follows. Finally, the *Galerie du bord de l'eau* or Great Gallery, planned by Catherine de Médicis and built by Clément Métezeau and Jacques Androuet du Cerceau between 1595 and 1607, occupies the western portion of the building.

On the eastern side of the Louvre is the royal entrance and the principal façade, constructed in the classical style which was inspired by 17th-century rationalism. It bears little resemblance to the rest of the building. The lower part of the façade is simple and severe. The upper part bears the colossal colonnade which gives the structure its name.

The **Colonnade** was begun in 1667 but work was suspended when Louis XIV transferred his court to Versailles, ending the history of the Louvre as the residence of the king. The project for an exposed basement surrounded by large moats was realised only recently, between 1964 and 1967. The new moats, 25m wide and 7.5m deep, give the Colonnade greater thrust and, for the first time, place the elements of the façade in proper proportion.

From the central arches of the Colonnade one enters the Cour Carrée, the great square courtyard whose walls bear the seals of the French kings.

The west façade is the oldest and most interesting. The part between the Pavillon de l'Horloge and the southern wing was built by Pierre Lescot between 1546 and 1549. Wide, covered arcades characterise the ground floor; large windows, the first floor; statues and reliefs executed by Jean Goujon and his workshop decorate the attic storey. Perhaps the richest sculptural decoration is in the three curvilinear pediments, where allegorical figures and pagan gods celebrate the renaissance themes of war and peace, fame and science.

Jacques Lemercier designed the northern part of the façade and the Pavillon de l'Horloge in 1624. The other three walls, planned after the example of the west wall, are largely the work of Le Vau (1660-1664) but were completed by Percier and Fontaine.

Today the national museum of the Louvre contains one of the world's most comprehensive collections of ancient Egyptian, Middle Eastern, Greek and Roman art, as well as an extensive body of European painting and sculpture.

The collection was begun by Francis I. It grew under Louis XIII and Louis XIV, mainly under the influence of Colbert, the powerful finance minister.

It was opened to the public in 1793. Today it includes nearly 300,000 catalogued pieces. At least two visits are recommended for the visitor intending to look at the galleries in any detail. The museum is divided into six sections: Greek and Roman antiquity, ancient Egyptian art, ancient Oriental art, medieval and modern sculpture, the royal treasure with a collection of precious objects, and medieval and modern painting. There is space in this book for only a handful of the masterpieces housed in the museum and the selection can scarcely be more than a token representation.

The Louvre possesses one of the great collections of Greek and Roman art including the justly famous *Winged Victory of Samothrace* and the *Venus de Milo*. The former is displayed in a most dramatic fashion at the top of the Daru staircase.

Probably the most celebrated painting in the world is the *Mona Lisa* which Leonardo painted between 1503 and 1506. The *Mona Lisa* introduced a new format in portrait painting which was used until the 19th century. Previous portraits had concentrated on the head and shoulders of the figure, cutting the body at mid-chest.

Leonardo's *Mona Lisa*

Leonardo continues the composition well below the waist, creating a sense of majesty similar to that of full-length portraits.

The calm, delicate smile of the subject has inspired men for centuries. Its suggestion of serene unconcern for worldly matters sets the subject apart from common mortals.

Also by Leonardo, who was the first Italian artist to be invited to France by Francis I, are the *Virgin of the Rocks* and the *Virgin and St Anne*. There are two versions of the *Virgin of the Rocks:* one in the National Gallery of London and one here in the Louvre. This panel is earlier and executed entirely by Leonardo, whereas the London painting is largely the work of his pupils. The landscape background is an important feature of this work. Dark and menacing rock formations provide an immediate backdrop to the figures. Soft light and delicate shades of blue and green delineate the more distant background. The scale and composition of the *Virgin and Saint Anne* had a deep and immediate influence on Florentine artists. The figures intertwine to form a single group animated by gestures and by the emotive relationship explicit in the facial expressions.

This painting is the subject of a famous essay by Freud which interprets the relationship between the two mothers in terms of that between Leonardo's real mother and his stepmother.

Among the paintings by Raphael at the Louvre are *La Belle Jardinière* of 1507 and the *Saint Michael and the Dragon* of 1518. The earlier painting was done while Raphael was still working in Florence. It is particularly notable for the harmony and serenity of the composition and the calm beauty of the subject. The *Saint Michael* was a gift to Francis I from Pope Leo X.

The two *Prisoners* by Michelangelo are a priceless addition to the collection. The *Prisoners* are unfinished pieces originally intended to form part of the monumental tomb of Pope Julius II in Rome. The tomb was never finished, and the two *Prisoners* of the Louvre (four more are preserved in Florence) were given by Michelangelo to Roberto Strozzi. During his exile in France, Strozzi presented the statues to Henry II in 1550.

The precise meaning of the *Prisoners* has never been determined. Vasari believed them to be the provinces captured by the warrior Pope. Modern critics associate them with the torment of earthly existence, to be ended by heavenly release.

The *Deposion of Christ* and the *Four Evangelists* by Jean Goujon were executed between 1544 and 1545 under the direction of Pierre Lescot. These bas-reliefs were destined for the pulpit of the church of Saint-

The Hall of the Caryatids

Germain-l'Auxerrois which was demolished in 1745.

The **Hall of the Caryatids** and the Staircase of Henry II exemplify the past splendour of the renaissance Louvre, now lost through numerous restorations and alterations.

The interior of the renaissance palace was designed by Pierre Lescot and decorated by Jean Goujon. The Hall of the Caryatids takes its name from the four female figures by Goujon which hold up the orchestra platform at the far end of the room. The figures vaguely resemble the famous caryatids of the Erectheum in Athens, hence the name of the hall.

The monumental **Staircase of Henry II** leading from the Hall of the Caryatids to the first floor, where the guards' hall and the king's anteroom were once located, is one of the most beautiful remnants of the old palace. The sculptural decoration of the staircase, carved by Goujon, has remained almost intact.

The Arc de Triomphe du Carrousel

The Place du Carrousel

The area enclosed by the two great arms of the Louvre is called the **Place du Carrousel.** The name derives from the great carrousel of June 1662 held in honour of the birth of the Dauphin. A triumphal arch commemorating Napoleon's victories at Austerlitz, Ulm and Tilsit during the campaign of 1805 stands at the centre. The arch is an imitation of the arch of Septimius Severus in Rome. It was built by Denon between 1806 and 1808 on a plan drafted by Percier and Fontaine. It is 14.6m high, 19.5m wide and 8.75m deep.

The **Jardin des Tuileries** is the most famous park in Paris. It is almost one km long and stretches from Place du Carrousel to Place de la Concorde.

The garden was conceived at the same time as Catherine de Médicis', Tuileries Palace. It was open to the public in the same way the Italian parks of the aristocracy were. In 1664 Colbert commissioned André le Nôtre, the architect of the gardens of Versailles to harmonise the garden

The Jardin des Tuileries

with Le Vau's architecture. Le Nôtre fulfilled the task admirably, making the Tuileries one of the most beautiful French gardens.

At the bottom of the Jardin des Tuileries are two pavilions, the **Orangerie,** on the side of the river, and the **Jeu de Paume,** on the side of Rue de Rivoli. In the Orangerie there are only a few permanent paintings, but many important shows are held there. The Jeu de Paume, on the other hand, is the gallery of the Impressionists. Here are the most famous paintings of this great movement, from the early masterpieces by Manet such as *Déjeuner sur l'herbe* and *Olympia,* through the works of Monet, Renoir, etc. to the later works of Gauguin and Le Douanier Rousseau.

Manet's *Olympia* in the Jeu de Paume

Monet's *Gare Saint-Lazare* in the Jeu de Paume

The **Palais Royal,** across the Rue de Rivoli from the Louvre, constituted an active social, political and psychological guide to Paris and to the *ancien régime* for many years. Richelieu commissioned Jacques Lemercier in 1629 to construct the Palais-Cardinal, the forerunner of the Palais Royal on the site of the Hôtel d'Angennes. Richelieu died there in 1642, leaving the palace to his king, Louis XIII. Anne of Austria took possession of the building in 1643, and the palace was renamed the Palais Royal. Louis XIV donated the building to his brother, Philippe d'Orléans, since it held unpleasant associations for him after the time of the Fronde, the insurrections which took place during his childhood. Philippe II d'Orléans gave the palace its present appearance, and his son Louis Philippe added the wings surrounding the garden, which became a meeting place for Parisian society and played an important role in the Revolution.

One enters the main courtyard through the passageway which opens on to Rue de Valois. The **Galerie des proues,** on the side facing Rue de Valois, is all that remains of the original palace constructed by Richelieu. The rear wall of the palace dates from the 18th century. Pilasters are attached to the first floor wall-surface and sculptural decoration to the attic storey. The **Galerie d'Orléans,** a double colonnade with doric columns, built by Fontaine between 1829 and 1831, separates the courtyard from the garden. The garden, 225m long and 90m wide, was completely transformed between 1781 and 1784 by Louis Philippe, who commissioned Victor Louis to enclose it within three buildings with colossal columns. The ground floor of the buildings, an open arcade which extends around all three sides, was dedicated to business and entertainment, and today is occupied by art and antique shops, secondhand booksellers, and rare-stamp sellers. The porticos bear the names of the lesser branches of the Orléans family: Montpensier, Beaujolais and Valois.

The Galérie d'Orléans in the Palais Royal

Detail of the Place des Victoires

The Place des Victoires

At the end of the Rue des Petits Champs, behind the garden of the Palais Royal, is **Place des Victoires.** The ideological basis of the *places royales,* exemplified in Place Dauphine and des Vosges, initially reflected real social needs and responded to the problems posed by urban planning. But the later *places royales* – notably Place des Victoires, Place Vendôme and Place de la Concorde – depart from these ideological guidelines. They seem significant only to their architects, Jules Hadouin-Mansart in the case of Place des Victoires and Place Vendôme, and the later Jacques Ange-Gabriel for Place de la Concorde.

François d'Aubusson, duke of Le Feuillare, commissioned the project for Place des Victoires from Jules Hardouin-Mansart in 1685. The horseshoe-shaped square, sur-

rounded by buildings with a uniform façade, was completed in 1686. It originally contained Martin Dejardin's statue of Louis XIV, lighted by four monumental lamps, but the statue was destroyed during the Revolution, though the pedestal reliefs are preserved in the Louvre. The four lamps were bitterly criticised and soon removed. François-Joseph Bosio executed the present equestrian statue, erected in 1822.

The urban reconstruction of the 19th century destroyed the architectural unity of Place des Victoires, leaving the disfigured square we see today.

The **Place Vendôme,** which can be reached from Rue de la Paix or from Rue de Castiglione, was originally called Place Louis le Grand. The original project, commissioned from Jules Hardouin-Mansart in 1687, proposed what today would be called a 'cultural centre', incorporating the statue of Louis XIV executed in 1692 by Girardon. But Mansart changed the original plan and built the present octagonal square between 1701 and 1720, when it became clear that the available funds were not sufficient to finance the construction of the more ambitious project.

On 15 August 1810 Napoleon I installed the famous triumphal column in Place Vendôme. The monument, 43.5m high, is an imitation of Trajan's Column in Rome. The bas-reliefs, which celebrate the emperor's victories between 1805 and 1807, were cast with the bronze from more than 1200 Russian and Austrian cannons captured at Austerlitz. A statue of Napoleon dressed as Caesar, executed by Augustin Dumont in 1863, stands at the top of the column.

Leaving Place Vendôme by Rue de Castiglione and turning right down Rue Saint Honoré, on the right is the church of **Saint-Roch.** In 1653 the fourteen year old Louis XIV laid the first stone of this church, one of Paris's more notable baroque monu-

The church of Saint-Roch

Saint-Roch, the nativity group in the Chapel of the Virgin

ments. The church was the religious centre of a wealthy parish, that of the Palais Royal and of Place Vendôme.

Saint-Roch was begun under the direction of Jacques Lemercier. The church is 35m wide and 125m long – almost as long as Notre-Dame. The nave, chapels, transept and chancel were completed in 1690. Jules Hardouin-Mansart resumed work at the beginning of the 18th century, erecting the domed Chapel of the Virgin, at the end of the chancel, between 1706 and 1710, and the Chapel of Communion, between the arms of the ambulatory, in 1717. The vaults of the nave, choir and transept were completed in 1722 and Robert de Cotte constructed the façade in 1736.

The sculpture in Saint-Roch (particularly the elaborate monumental tombs) make the church among the most interesting of repositories of 17th-century French art. The marble nativity group on the main altar of the Chapel of the Virgin comes from the church of Val-de-Grâce. It was executed in 1625 by François and Michel Anguier.

The statue of Joan of Arc in Place des Pyramides

The absenteeism of the king, the disastrous wars of Louis XVI, the perpetual unrest surrounding the rationing of food, the drop in wages and rise in unemployment that followed the Anglo-French trade agreement of 1716, all contributed to the outbreak of the French Revolution.

The Revolution began on 14 July 1789 with the fall of the Bastille, the fortress built by Charles V between 1369 and 1382 and used as a prison by Charles VI. Under Richelieu it was definitively transformed into a prison for political prisoners. But by 1789 the Bastille no longer held any political prisoners, nor was it of any strategic importance. It remained, however, the symbol of absolute power and as such the focal point of the citizens' anger. The following year it was completely destroyed and the square we see now, Place de la Bastille, was built in 1803. The column in the centre is called the **Colonne de Juillet** and was set up in 1840 to commemorate the Parisians killed during the revolution of July 1830 against the Bourbons.

The events which followed the fall of the Bastille all took place in the streets and palaces of the capital. Much of Paris' artistic heritage – particularly those monuments which represented the kings – was destroyed.

The period following the Revolution was one of unprecedented growth for Paris; at the time of the First Empire the city's population numbered more than 500,000. Public and private building flourished. Napoleon entrusted the work of city planning and the construction of monuments to Percier and Fontaine, whose numerous works include the triumphal arches of the Étoile and the Carrousel, the Madeleine and Rue de Rivoli.

In 1853, two years after the advent of Napoleon III, the population of Paris reached 1,200,000. This extraordinary growth, together with the political needs of the regime of Napoleon III and the middle classes' fear of further revolts, like those that brought about the downfall of Charles X in 1830 and of Louis Philippe in 1848, led Napoleon III, in the third quarter of the century, to order a comprehensive plan of urban renewal. This plan, carried out by his prefect, Baron Haussmann, is *'the first example of a city planning programme extended over the entire body of a city and carried out in a coherent way over a relatively brief period of time'* (Benevolo).

Haussmann's plans called for the construction of new residential areas on the outskirts of Paris; the building of wide, straight boulevards which could be used for the rapid movement of troops from one part of the city to another; the creation of public parks (namely, the Bois de Boulogne, the Bois de Vincennes, the Buttes-Chaumont and Parc Montsouris); the renewal and extension of public services (water, gas, waste disposal and urban transport); the reorganisation of the bureaucracy and the establishment of laws governing construction.

The construction of new buildings along the grands boulevards was carefully controlled and, in some cases the façade was erected before the rest of the building. The general principle that governed the recomposition of the city seems to have been the application, on a larger scale, of the concepts of regularity and symmetry developed by the architects of the *places royales*. The large open spaces and monumental perspectives created by Haussmann and his engineers made Paris one of the most modern and beautiful cities of the 19th century.

Paris' Napoleonic monuments – the Arc de Triomphe du Carrousel, the Arc de Triomphe de l'Étoile, the column of Place Vendôme and others – are carefully placed in the architectural environment of the *ancien régime*. The **Madeleine** is placed with similar care on the northern arm of an enormous symbolic cross whose

The church of the Madeleine

Coysevox's statue of Mercury in the Place de la Concorde

The Palais-Bourbon

major axis runs from the Arc du Carrousel to that of the Étoile and whose southern arm terminates at the Palais-Bourbon, on the left bank of the Seine.

The Madeleine was built on the site of an unfinished church, also dedicated to St Mary Magdalen, which was demolished in 1806. The present structure was begun by Pierre Alexandre Vignon and completed by Huvé. It was consecrated in 1814.

The Madeleine was designed to be a temple of military glory, and is modelled on the temples of ancient Greece. A grandiose colonnade surrounds the central hall and the principal façade terminates in a richly sculptured pediment representing the *Last Judgment*. The interior is a single, large hall with a semicircular apse. Marble sculpture groups from the Napoleonic period decorate the entrance vestibule and the main altar.

In Place des Pyramides, not far down the Rue de Rivoli from Place de la Concorde, is the statue of *Joan of Arc* by Frémiet (1874). The statue is placed here because, according to the legend, this is where the maid of Orléans was wounded during the siege of Paris.

Place de la Concorde, dedicated to Louis XV, is the last and most splendid of the *place royales*. It was built on a tract of abandoned land along the Seine between the Jardin des Tuileries and the western boundary of the city. It was designed and built by Jacques Ange-Gabriel between 1760 and 1775.

The original square was surrounded by moats and by a balustrade interrupted at regular intervals by eight small ornamental pavilions. Bouchardon's statue of Louis XV stood at the centre, but was destroyed in 1796. The Obelisk of Ramses II, a gift from Mehmet Ali to Louis Philippe, replaced the destroyed statue in 1836. The construction of two large fountains, designed by Hittorf and modelled after those in St Peter's Square in Rome, completed the decoration of the square. Two equestrian statues by Coysevox, which originally marked the entrance to the Champs Elysées, were transferred to the entrance to the Jardin des Tuileries in 1719, and the two large horses executed by Guillaume Coustou in 1733 for the castle of Marly have taken their place.

The **Palais-Bourbon,** on the other side of the Seine, was built between 1722 and 1728 for the duchess of Bourbon, the daughter of Louis XIV. It has been continually enlarged and reconstructed and is now the seat of the national assembly.

The principal façade was built by Poyet in 1807, in the same neo-classical style as the Madeleine. The lateral wings of the main courtyard are part of the pre-Revolutionary expansion carried out by the Prince of Condé.

The Fontaine des Quatre-Saisons

The monumental **Fontaine des Quatre-Saisons,** unfortunately standing in a street too narrow to do it justice, was decorated between 1739 and 1746 by Edmé Bouchardon, the famous sculptor of Versailles. The statues of the central structure represent the city of Paris overlooking the Seine and the Marne, which lie at its feet. The four seasons stand above allegorical bas-reliefs in the semicircular lateral wings.

The order and precision of the vast Esplanade des Invalides, designed by Robert de Cotte between 1704 and 1720, is a fitting precedent to the massive façade of the **Hôtel de Invalides.**

Louis XIV founded the Institution des Invalides on the grounds of Saint-Germain-des-Prés in 1670, to assist mutilated and invalid soldiers and to prevent their begging and loitering. The construction of the Institution was commissioned to Libéral Bruant, who erected the building between 1671 and 1676.

The austere appearance of the Hôtel des Invalides indicates a perfect correspondence between the building's aesthetic and utilitarian functions. In a sense, it is a masterpiece of the civilisation of the *grand siècle*. The façade, 210m long, clearly reveals the strict rationalism with which the modules of proportion

The courtyard of the Hôtel des Invalides

have been determined. The arched pediment of the monumental doorway interrupts the long roof line. Nevertheless, it carries on the rhythm established by the pediments of the corner pavilions and it echoes the arches of the ground floor doors and windows. The door interrupts the continuity by standing out slightly from the wall. But it also enhances that continuity, acting as a central counterpart to the pavilions and to the protruding surfaces which correspond to the axes of the internal courtyards.

The doorway leads directly to the main courtyard, which is surrounded by porticoes with proportions based on the radii of the arches. These are interrupted by four central pavilions, each surmounted by a triangular pediment.

Jules Hardouin-Mansart continued the construction of the Invalides after 1676. He is primarily responsible for the church of **Saint-Louis-des-Invalides** (70m long and 22m wide), which one enters from the centre of the southern arcade in the main courtyard.

From Saint-Louis-des-Invalides we pass through the Corridor of Metz, through a small courtyard and into the larger courtyard of the Dôme des Invalides.

The royal church of the **Dôme des**

Interior of the church of the Dôme des Invalides

Invalides, built between 1677 and 1706, is Jules Hardouin-Mansart's greatest achievement. The architect's contemporaries considered it an absolute exposition of the principles of French neoclassicism. Mansart's plan imposes an authoritarian rhythm on the whole construction. The façade rises vertically on tall doric and corinthian columns and expands horizontally through the movement established by the projecting pediments. Sculptural decorations are soberly inserted in the architectural framework. Statues of Charlemagne and Saint-Louis, executed by Antoine Coysevox, occupy the pediments.

The dome, covered by sheets of gold-coated lead and surmounted by a lantern and a pinnacle, rests on a bipartite drum. The drum's lower elevation is composed of windows with semicircular arches and a corbel table with vase motifs.

Inside the Dôme des Invalides is the **Tomb of Napoleon.** The ashes of Napoleon I were returned to Paris in 1840 from the island of St Helena. In 1843, the architect Visconti constructed a large, circular crypt in which the porphyry sarcophagus was deposited. The sarcophagus is 4m long, 2m wide and 4.5m high. It rests on a baseboard of green Vosges granite. Twelve colossal Victories, carved by Pradier, are attached to the surrounding columns.

The Tomb of Napoleon

IESV NASCENTI VIRGINIQ MATRI

The church of Val-de-Grâce

Another of Jules Hardouin-Mansart's masterpieces is the church of **Val-de-Grâce.** The construction was decided by Anne of Austria who gave birth to the future Louis XIV in 1638, after a long period of doubt and anticipation. During this period she vowed to build a church on the site of the convent of the Benedictine nuns who had consoled her during that time. Louis XIV himself laid the foundation stone of the new building in 1645. Jules Hardouin-Mansart designed the church and its construction was begun by Jacques Lemercier and completed by Pierre Le Muet and Gabriel Le Duc. The dome, 40m high, is the work of Le Muet and Le Duc. Le Duc had lived in Rome and had studied the baroque monuments of Bernini: the baldachin above the main altar is an imitation of Bernini's baldachin in St Peter's. A painting by Pierre Mignard, representing the Glory of the Blessed, occupies the ceiling of the dome.

The Val-de-Grâce is the only Parisian convent which has remained unchanged since the 17th century. The church was re-opened in 1828 and transformed into a chapel for the military hospital installed on the site in 1755.

Walking back towards the river along the Rue Saint-Jacques, on the right is the Place du Panthéon. Jacques-Germain Soufflot began the **Panthéon** in 1756, and died without seeing it completed. This grandiose monument was finished during the first years of the Revolution. It is 110m long, 82m wide and 83m high, under the lantern of the dome. It is built in the form of a Greek cross.

The Panthéon is located on Mont Sainte-Geneviève, on the site of the early Christian basilica in which the remains of Ste Geneviève were kept. An abbey was founded there and it soon became a sacred place for Christianity. It retained its fame throughout the Middle Ages, rivalling Saint-Germain-des-Prés in importance.

The Panthéon was originally planned as a basilica dedicated to St Germain but it became a temple of national glory in 1791 (Mirabeau, Voltaire and Rousseau are buried there). It was reconsecrated by Napoleon III, but reverted to its secular function when the ashes of Victor Hugo were placed there in 1885.

The interior of the Panthéon

The church of Saint-Sulpice

Near the Panthéon, down Rue Soufflot and along Rue de Médicis, is the **Palais du Luxembourg** with its garden. Although a much older construction originally, this palace was bought in 1612 by Maria de Médicis, the mother of Louis XIII, who commissioned the architect Salomon de Brosse to build her a palace and a park which would remind her of Italy. During the Revolution the palace was used as a prison, and it was Napoleon who designated it as seat of the Senate, which it still is today.

The cycle of 21 paintings by Rubens illustrating the life of Maria de Médicis and now in the Louvre, were originally painted for a gallery in this palace.

The new church of **Saint-Sulpice,** in Place Saint Sulpice, was built on the site of a pre-existent church dating from the 12th century. It was begun by Gamard in 1646. His successor, Daniel Gittard, built the chancel between 1660 and 1678. Oppenord and Servandoni completed the transept and built the nave between 1719 and 1736, and Servandoni began the façade in 1733.

Servandoni's façade is divided into two levels bearing doric and ionic columns. It terminates in two towers, 73 and 68m high. The interior is 110m long, 56m wide and 33m high. Delacroix painted the compositions representing *Saint Michael and the Devil* (in the vault) and *The Expulsion of Heliodorus* and *The Last*

Holy-water font in Saint-Sulpice

Judgment (on the walls), in 1853.

The **Palais de l'Institut de France,** on the Quai de Conti near the Pont des Arts, was built when Mazarin ordered the foundation of a college in Paris for 60 students from the four regions annexed to France by the Treaty of the Pyrénées, and Louis Le Vau drafted the general plans for the Collège des Quatre Nations in 1662. The building was erected between 1662 and 1688 under the direction of Lambert and François d'Orbay. The Institut de France, created in 1795, took possession of the building in 1806 and it now houses the five academies of the Institut, the most important of which is the Académie Française, founded by Richelieu in 1635.

Le Vau's palace, designed in the style of the Roman baroque, revolves around a central structure (originally a chapel) surmounted by a tall, graceful dome. Two semicircular columnated wings link the chapel to the two lateral pavilions.

The Palais de l'Institut de France

The **Opéra,** between Boulevard Haussmann and Boulevard des Capucines, is the largest and, perhaps, the most famous opera house in the world. The broad Avenue de l'Opéra, located at the centre of Paris' business district, links it to the city's monumental centre (the Louvre, the Tuileries and the Palais Royal).

Jean-Louis-Charles Garnier planned the monumental theatre (his only work) after winning a competition in 1861. Construction began immediately and ended in 1875.

The Opéra is, in every sense, a theatrical structure. Architecture and decoration are indivisible: paintings, sculpture, mosaics and furniture blend with, and give meaning to, the architectural elements. Further, a precise relationship exists between the interior and exterior of the building. The vestibule corresponds to the arcades of the peristyle; the large foyer corresponds to the columnated upper porch of the façade, which is reached by way of a monumental staircase. Mythological and allegorical themes (Apollo and the Muses; Poetry, Music and Dance) are developed in a profusion of paintings and mosaics. A broad dome covers the auditorium, which seats 2158. The pediment above the stage, described by Garnier as *'immense, developpé arrêtant les regards et faisant, pour ainsi dire, le fond du tableau'*, bears statues of Apollo, Poetry and Music. The stage is among the largest in Europe: it is 52m wide, 60m high and 37m deep.

The rear part of the building contains the administrative offices, the stage entrance and the dance foyer. The Pavilion of Honour, designed for Napoleon III, now houses the museum and library of the Opéra. It is located on the left side of the building.

Façade of the Opéra

POESIE LYRIQUE
DE MUSIQUE
STATIONNEMENT
GENANT

Interior of the dome of Saint-Augustin

On the Boulevard Haussmann, between the Opéra and Place Saint Augustin, is Place Louis XVI with the **Chapelle Expiatoire.** This chapel was built between 1815 and 1826 by Fontaine on the site where the victims of the guillotine were buried.

The curious church of **Saint-Augustin,** in the square of the same name, was designed by Victor Baltard, the architect of the demolished pavilions of Les Halles, and built between 1860 and 1871. Auguste Perret considered Saint-Augustin an important example of that part of 19th-century architecture which, through the use of iron, paved the way for the development of modern architecture.

The extraordinarily light cast iron framework of the nave and dome is Baltard's greatest contribution to architectural development. The part of the building constructed in stone is a mixture of renaissance and byzantine motifs.

The church is oriented towards the north and is trapezoid in form rather than rectangular. Its odd shape is in part determined by the fan-like arrangement of the side chapels. In the crypt are the remains of Napoleon III.

St Michael of Farnborough in Hampshire, England, is an exact replica of Saint-Augustin.

The church of Saint-Augustin

Avenue Foch leading to the Arc de Triomphe de l'Étoile

Paolo Uccello: *St George and the Dragon* in the Musée Jacquemart-André

From Place Saint Augustin along the Boulevard Haussmann is the **Musée Jaquemart-André** which houses French and Italian works of art from the 15th to the 18th centuries. Particularly worthy of mention are the paintings by Carpaccio and Paolo Uccello.

At the end of Boulevard Haussmann is Place Charles de Gaulle, known more commonly as the **Étoile.** The large circus with the Arc de Triomphe at the centre, was conceived by Baron Haussmann in 1854. In Haussmann's plan, the Place appears as the hub of an immense wheel whose five spokes were to be major arteries of the new, systematically planned city. Jacques-Ignace Hittorff, the designer of the buildings that surround the Étoile, altered Haussmann's plan, changing the number of axes from five to twelve. The present form of the Étoile is principally the work of Hittorff. At the end of the 18th century, the Étoile was little more than the summit of the hill of Chaillot, the point of convergence of the Champs-Élysées and five other wide avenues which led to the new neighbourhoods erected on the outskirts of the city. In 1806 Napoleon I commissioned Jean-François Chalgain to build a large triumphal arch at the Étoile, as a monument to the glory of his *grande armée*. Its construction, like that of many monuments of the Napoleonic era, dragged on for years. It was finally completed in 1836.

The **Arc de Triomphe** is 14.5m high, 44.8m wide and 22.2m deep. The only interesting part of its profuse sculptural decoration is the relief representing the *Departure of the Volunteers in 1792,* commonly called the *Marseillaise,* carved by François Rude in 1835-1836.

The view from the top of the Arc de Triomphe includes some of Haussmann's more noteworthy achievements: Avenue Foch, 1300m long and 120m wide, connects the Étoile to the Bois de Boulogne, the immense park created by Haussmann and Alphand in 1852.

The relief of the *Marseillaise* on the Arc de Triomphe

The Cascades in the Bois de Boulogne

Paris after 1870

Paris was a different city when Haussmann left office in 1870. The population had increased to nearly two million inhabitants, the city's appearance was completely transformed and its administration and services renewed.

The industrial revolution effectively destroyed this momentary equilibrium. By the end of the century it was already clear that Haussmann's plans for development were inadequate for confronting the problems posed by Paris' rapid expansion. The metropolis spread with amazing speed into the surrounding countryside as outlying villages were industrialized or transformed into working class residential areas. The growth of industrial activity on the outskirts of Paris contributed to a depopulation of the city's centre. A lack of adequate roadways complicated the circulation of traffic. The construction of the Métro in the last decade of the 19th century and the multiplication of bus lines and taxis made communication between one part of the city and another easier but compounded the traffic problem.

The Exhibitions of 1878, 1889 and 1900 made Paris the centre of world attention. These Exhibitions became showcases of the new developments of the industrial revolution. Steel, glass and reinforced concrete, the fundamental elements of 20th-century architecture, were used with increasing frequency, both in the temporary pavilions of the Exhibitions and in the public and private architecture of industrialised Paris. At the same time, the city became the cultural and artistic centre of Europe. Increasing numbers of French and foreigners invaded the university, the theatres, concerts, expositions, department stores, music halls and cafés of Montmartre and Montparnasse.

The Palais de Chaillot from the Eiffel Tower

View of the Champ de Mars from the terrace of the Palais de Chaillot

The hill of Chaillot is located between the Bois de Boulogne and the Seine, in the elegant residential district of the 10th arrondissement. It is the last of the chain of hills – originally populated by villages, abbeys and monasteries – which extends westward in a long arch from Montmartre to the Seine.

Napoleon I envisaged the hill of Chaillot as the site of a new and extraordinary palace which was to dominate Paris from the end of the Champs-Elysées. His project was never realised. Nevertheless, the dream was not allowed to dissolve entirely, for it was born of the same sense of historic destiny which underlay the vast 19th century projects of urban renewal and city planning: the colossal but brief Exhibitions of the late 19th century expressed the historic dream of the *ville lumière* in new forms, in economic and technological terms; the Exhibition of 1878 led to the construction of the fabulous Palais du Trocadéro, and this in turn was replaced by the present **Palais de Chaillot,** built for the Exhibition of 1937 by the architects Jacques Carlu, Boileau and Azéma.

The palace, facing Palais du Trocadéro, consists of two monumental pavilions separated by a terrace, and two curved wings 195m long. These embrace a complex of gardens, ramps, terraces and paths which slope gently toward the Seine.

The eastern pavilion houses the **Musée des Monuments Français,** dedicated to French monumental art. The collection contains copies of sculpture and mural paintings from the Carolingian period to the 19th century. The gothic sculpture section includes reproductions of the sculptural programmes of the cathedrals of Chartres, Amiens and Reims.

The western pavilion houses the **Musée de la Marine,** a museum of maritime history, and the **Musée de l'Homme.** The latter is one of the world's larger museums of anthro-

Palais d'Art Moderne

pology, prehistory and ethnology. It includes exhibitions of physical anthropology and human palaeontology, as well as a vast collection of art, costumes, tools and arms from all parts of the world.

In the Place d'Iéna (named in honour of a Napoleonic victory) is the **Musée Guimet** which houses an extraordinary collection of oriental art. Works from China, Tibet, India, Japan and other eastern countries are displayed here.

Nearby on the Avenue Wilson is the **Palais d'Art Moderne.** It was built for the Exhibition of 1937. The outside of the Palace is decorated with numerous pieces of sculpture and bas-reliefs; probably the most famous is the statue of *France* (1927) by Bourdelle. Inside, paintings by such celebrated modernists as Matisse, Picasso, Braque, Chagall and Salvador Dali are to be found in the west wing. In the east wing one finds the Museum of the City of Paris and Costumes of the City of Paris.

Picasso: *L'Aubade* 1942, in the Palais d'Art Moderne

Braque: *The Bird and his Nest* 1956, in the Palais d'Art Moderne

Léger: *Blue Ballerina* 1930, in the Palais d'Art Moderne

The Maison de l'ORTF, headquarters of French television

Also on the Avenue Wilson one finds the **Palais du Conseil Economique et Social,** one of Auguste Perret's more harmonious works. The building, originally designed as a museum of public works, was built in 1937-1938. The framework of reinforced concrete is used in conjunction with a style of architecture which attempts to avoid the repetition of motifs used in the past.

Paralleling the Seine in the direction of the Maison de Radio-France, the beautiful modern headquarters of French television

51-55, Rue Raynouard, designed by Auguste Perret

25bis, Rue Franklin, designed by Auguste Perret

which are well worth a visit, is a long road with splendid private buildings. At **25 bis, Rue Franklin** is an apartment building, built by Auguste and Gustave Perret in 1903, the first in Paris to be constructed of reinforced concrete.

The Rue Franklin then becomes the **Rue Raynouard** and at **51-55** Auguste Perret built an apartment which he lived in until the end of his life.

Castel Béranger, designed by Hector Guimard

Changing names once again the street becomes the Rue La Fontaine. Here are some particularly well known houses such as No 14, the famous **Castel-Béranger**. This was built in 1897-1898 by Hector Guimard. It is a major example of art nouveau.

The group of apartment houses which includes Nos 17, 19 and 21 Rue La Fontaine and Nos 8 and 10 Rue Agar were all built by Hector Guimard in 1911. They clearly establish Guimard as a master of art nouveau.

The **Eiffel Tower** is, perhaps more than any other monument, the symbol of Paris. It was built by the engineer, Gustave Eiffel, for the Exhibition of 1889. Many 'respectable' Parisians opposed its construction, for they believed it destroyed the harmony of the city's appearance. Robert Delauney, Raymond Duchamp-Villon, Antoine Pevsner, Naum Gabo and Le Corbusier, noted figures of the 20th-century artistic vanguard, were the first to realise its value, which rests mainly in Eiffel's treatment of open spaces, conceived in terms of overlapping lines and force fields.

The tower is 320m high and weighs 7000 tonnes. It is made up of over 15,000 pieces of steel, and horizontal platforms divide it into three parts. Restaurants and bars are located on the first two levels; lift and stairs serve all three levels. The view from the top of the tower is breathtaking: the visibility on a clear day exceeds 50km.

From the Eiffel Tower, crossing the Champ de Mars, the visitor can reach the **Ecole Militaire,** an interesting example of 18th-century French architecture, built between 1752 and 1772 by Jacques-Ange Gabriel for the military academy founded by Louis XV in 1751. Napoleon was a cadet at this school in 1784-1785. The entrance to the Cour d'Honneur of the academy is from Place de Fontenoy.

Also in Place de Fontenoy is the **UNESCO** building, built between 1955 and 1958 by the American architect Breuer, the French Zehrfuss and the Italian Nervi.

The building, which is Y-shaped, is enhanced by works of art by such great contemporary artists as Picasso, Mirò, Henry Moore, Calder, Tomayo and others.

The Eiffel Tower

The Ecole Militaire

Joan Miró, *Wall of the sun* (1958), UNESCO

Rodin: *Fugit Amor* in the Musée Rodin

Detail of the bronze decoration of the Pont-Alexandre-III

Pont-Alexandre-III

In the Rue de Varennes, off the Boulevard des Invalides, is the **Musée Rodin.** This museum is housed in the 18th-century Hôtel Biron and contains most of Rodin's most famous works: *The Thinker, The Kiss* and others.

The **Pont-Alexandre-III** is a single metal arch 107.5m long and 40m wide. Tsar Nicholas II laid the first stone; the engineers Résac and Alby completed the bridge in 1900.

Allegorical and naturalistic motifs cast in bronze decorate the central span, the corner piers, the monumental lamps and the parapets.

The Grand Palais

Crossing the Seine by the Pont-Alexander-III one arrives at the **Grand Palais** which was built for the Exhibition of 1900 by the architects Daglance, Louvet and Thomas under the direction of Charles Girault. Its massive proportions and profuse decoration exemplify the eclectic and rhetorical ideals of official French art at the turn of the century (note, for example the enormous bronze quadrigae symbolising Harmony dominating Discord, and Immortality preceding Time, which stand on top of the pavilions at the corners facing the Cours-la-Reine and the Champs-Élysées). The palace now houses the Galeries Nationales du Grand Palais, used principally for commercial exhibitions.

A bronze quadriga above a corner pavilion of the Grand Palais

The western part of the building includes the **Palais de la Découverte,** a museum of natural and applied sciences. It is divided into nine sections: physics, biology, optics, chemistry, medicine, nuclear physics, mathematics, astronomy and the history of science. Visitors may operate numerous instruments. The museum also offers demonstrations of simple experiments and documentary films. The adjacent planetarium presents daily lectures.

Across the Avenue Churchill from the Grand Palais is the **Petit Palais** which was also built by Girault for the Exhibition of 1900. This building is richly decorated but far more

Façade of the Petit Palais

Bonnard: *Nu dans la baignoire* 1937, in the Petit Palais

classical in design than its larger neighbour.

On the other side of the Champs-Élysées, on the corner of Avenue de Marigny and Rue du Fauborg Saint-Honoré, is the **Palais de l'Elysée,** the residence of the president of the republic. Since it was first built in the early 18th century, many great names of French history have lived here: Madame de Pompadour, Caroline Murat and Josephine Beauharnais. It was in this palace that Napoleon signed his abdication after the battle of Waterloo.

The tree-lined **Avenue des Champs-Élysées** extends from the Place de la Concorde to the Étoile. Its eastern end was constructed by Le Nôtre in 1667 and named Grand-Cours. The name was changed to Champs-Élysées in 1709. The Duke d'Antin, director of the royal gardens, extended the avenue to the Étoile in 1724.

The surrounding area was a favourite residence of the aristocracy during the Second Empire. Today the area has lost its aristocratic flavour. It has become a centre for some of Paris's better shops, travel agencies, restaurants, cafés and cinemas.

The **Théâtre des Champs-Élysées** is the first theatre built entirely in reinforced concrete. The initial plans of Henri Van der Velde were modified by Auguste and Gustave Perret, who built the theatre between 1911 and 1913. The sculptor Antoine Bordelle decorated the façade. Maurice Denis frescoed the ceiling of the hall of the Grand Théâtre and Edouard Vuillard painted the foyer of the Comédie.

The Théâtre des Champs-Élysées was one of the sacred places of modern dance. It was the site of the first famous performance of Stravinsky's *Rite of Spring* which caused an uproar that ended with actual rioting.

The quarter of **Montmartre** was the home of some of Paris's legendary painters, poets and lyricists, and it continues to contrast strongly with the city that surrounds it.

Montmartre is situated on a hill (the Butte Montmartre) 130m high, at the northern end of the city. The hilltop was originally the site of a Roman temple dedicated to Mercury. The Roman name for the hill, *Mons Mercurii,* may be a root of the present name. But Montmartre is also an important element in the legend of St Denis, the first bishop of Paris. He was martyred on the hill AD 272, and it was subsequently called *Mons Martyrum* which is probably a more likely source of its present name.

A Benedictine monastery grew up on Montmartre during the Middle Ages. Numerous windmills, which used the high winds there to grind grain were also built. Montmartre was a quiet country village until the end of the 18th century. Its population increased during the first 30 years of the 19th century as the city began to expand toward the north. The hill entered violently into modern history in 1871 when it provided an extremely valuable military

Utrillo: *Maison Bernot in Montmartre* in the Orangerie

position throughout the period of the Paris Commune. In the following years, the workers employed in the construction of the church of the Sacré-Cœur began to inhabit the area. Rents were low enough to encourage many workers from the surrounding countryside to live there. The same low rents attracted Paris's poorer artists and literary figures (those who had already acquired some wealth settled in the new quarters of the city, principally in Nouvelle Athènes). Corot, Renoir, van Gogh, Toulouse-Lautrec, Picasso and Utrillo have contributed greatly to the fame of Montmartre. Much of the quarter remains as they painted it 50 to 100 years ago.

The massive white dome of the **Sacré-Cœur** dominates the picturesque streets surrounding Place du Tertre, the central square of Montmartre. The church was erected by order of the national assembly. Construction began in 1873 and the completed building was consecrated on 16 October 1919. The first director of the project was Paul Abadie, but Daument, Laisné and Rauline each directed the construction at later stages.

The enormous, much debated structure reflects romanesque and byzantine styles. It is 100m long and 50m wide. The dome rises to a height of 83m, the bell tower to 84m. Four smaller domes surround the central one.

The grandiose interior is overloaded by excessive decoration – mosaics, sculpture and stained glass.

Historically the church of **Saint-Pierre de Montmartre** belongs to the earliest period of Paris's history, geographically, to the latest. The church is all that remains of the Benedictine monastery of Montmartre founded in 1133 by Adelaide de Savoie, the wife of Louis VI. The church is one of Paris's oldest gothic monuments. It was consecrated by Pope Eugenius II on Easter Monday, 1147. The sanctuary

The basilica of the Sacré-Coeur

Street scene in Montmartre with the dome of the Sacré-Coeur

contains the earliest examples of the pointed arch (a distinguishing feature of the gothic style) in Paris. The small apses, transept and the adjacent bay of the nave were all built before 1147. The larger main apse and the first three bays of the nave date from the end of the 12th century. The vaulting of the nave was completed in the 15th century.

Four columns from the original Temple of Mercury are to be found in the sanctuary, and on the interior of the nave façade.

The view of Paris from the hill of Montmartre, and especially from the dome of the Sacré-Coeur, is probably the best way of understanding the development of historic Paris.

Index